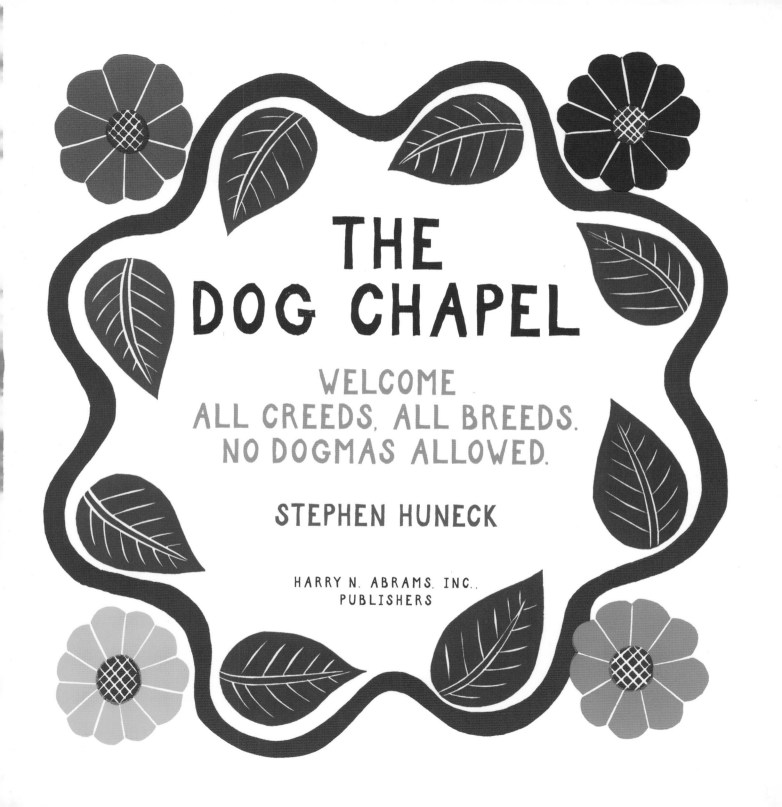

THE DOG CHAPEL

WELCOME
ALL CREEDS, ALL BREEDS.
NO DOGMAS ALLOWED.

STEPHEN HUNECK

HARRY N. ABRAMS, INC.,
PUBLISHERS

Project Manager: Howard W. Reeves
Editor: Susan Homer
Designer: Lindgren/Fuller Design
Production Director: Hope Koturo
Photography: Paul O. Boisvert

Library of Congress Cataloging-in-Publication Data

Huneck, Stephen.
The Dog chapel: welcome all creeds, all breeds. No dogmas allowed / by Stephen Huneck.
p. cm.
ISBN 0-8109-3488-4
1. Huneck, Stephen—Themes, motives. 2. Dogs in art. 3. Dog Chapel
(Saint Johnsbury, Vt.) 4. Dogs—Anecdotes. I. Title.
N6537.H78 A4 2002
704.9'4329772—dc21   2002003214

Printed and bound in Hong Kong
10 9 8 7 6 5 4 3 2 1

Harry N. Abrams, Inc.
100 Fifth Avenue
New York, N.Y. 10011
www.abramsbooks.com

Abrams is a subsidiary of
LA MARTINIÈRE
G R O U P E

To Sally

Sally, my very dear friend and constant companion, died not long ago. She was an eleven-year-old black Lab. Her passing was sudden and unexpected. It broke my heart, but I know we will always be together. This book is dedicated to all of the good times we shared.

PREFACE

Several years ago I became seriously ill. On my way to my studio, my arms full of the day's work, I slipped and went crashing down the stairs. I broke a couple of ribs and, without warning, fell victim to Adult Respiratory Distress Syndrome. In a coma for two months, I was given little chance of survival by my doctors. My wife, Gwen, refused to believe that I was not going to make it. She never left my side.

One evening the doctors told her that they didn't expect me to live through the night. I did have a very tough time that night and, in fact, stopped breathing for five minutes. In those five minutes, I had a profound experience, one that altered the course of my life forever. Though I came out of the coma two weeks later (to everyone's surprise but Gwen's), that night I had what is called a near-death experience.

This is what I remember. I got out of bed and found myself walking around the grounds of the hospital. I came upon an old, low, white clapboard building that looked like a very long stable. Altogether, there must have been fifty stalls, each one with a big door. Drawn to one door in particular, I opened it and entered. Inside the stall, I felt a strong presence. Slowly, as my eyes adjusted to the light, I was amazed to see a sculpture standing in the middle of what was actually a very large room. This sculpture wasn't just any sculpture. I sensed it was very, very old, and I knew a woman had created it. Awestruck, I could see its molecules pulsating with energy. Configured like a totem pole, its subject was the cycle of life—and remarkably, it seemed that it radiated life. There were all kinds of animals, some of them attacking and eating one another, some making love, others giving birth. I felt it was the greatest artwork I had ever seen. For in that moment, I understood perfectly how dying is a part of life.

Soon I realized that there was someone else in the room with me. In the darkness, I could clearly see the glimmer of his eyes, and just make out that it was a man with a dog's head. I called out to him. Perhaps, I thought, he was the sculpture's guardian. I told him I would give him everything I owned for the sculpture. Though he did not answer me verbally, I felt his response very clearly in my mind. He replied he would like for me to have the sculpture, for he had been looking for someone who appreciated it as much as he did. I wrote him a check for $43,000, all the money I had, and the sculpture was mine. Wow, was I excited!

When I awoke from the coma, I was fixated on the sculpture. Still on a respirator, I was unable to speak. I tried to write Gwen a note to tell her about my purchase and to make sure that we had enough money in our checking account to cover the check. However, to my great frustration, I had lost the use of all the muscles in my whole body, including my hand, and my writing was just scribbles. Looking back on this time, I have to laugh. Whenever doctors came into my room, I felt sure they were coming to tell me my check had bounced!

When I was well enough, our dogs, Sally and Dottie, came with Gwen to bring me home. What a love fest! The dogs understood my condition and stayed close. It was so wonderful to hug all my girls.

Once home, I had to rebuild my ravaged body and learn to walk again. My dogs were eager to help. They would walk on either side of me and urge me on as if I were their puppy. Sometimes they would run ahead with great bursts of speed and then stop and sit down, patiently waiting for me.

One day, not long after I got home, a wild idea just popped into my mind. (I have found that if wild ideas stick, no matter how crazy they may seem, I need to give them serious thought.) And the more I thought, the more I realized there was something I simply had to do. I wanted to build a chapel.

My chapel would celebrate the spiritual bond we have with our dogs, a place open to dogs and people of any faith or belief system. I envisioned building it on Dog Mountain, our mountaintop farm in St. Johnsbury, Vermont. I imagined it styled in the manner of a small, nineteenth-century village church built in Vermont. It was important to me that the Dog Chapel fit into its setting of rolling mountains and open fields. I imagined a white steeple pointing up to the heavens, and on the top, a golden Lab with wings.

I saw myself walking inside, bathed in the light of my stained-glass windows, dog carvings surrounding me, music playing. Everything was reaffirming the connection between art, nature, life, and love, all things for which I am truly grateful.

In 1997, I began construction. Since that time, I have made my dream come true. I have built the Dog Chapel. Inside, the windows offer messages my dogs have taught me about the nature of love, joy, friendship, play, trust, faith, and peace.

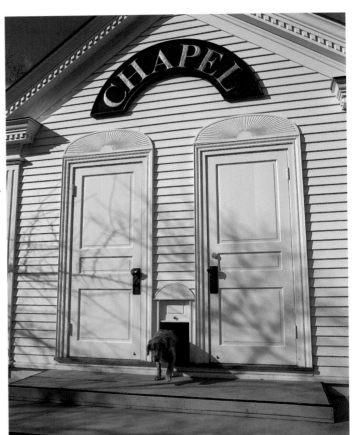

DOGS CAN HEEL...

DOGS CAN EVEN HEAL
A BROKEN HEART.

DO YOU EVER WONDER
IF GOD CREATED THE DOG
FOR THE CHILD OR THE CHILD
FOR THE DOG?

A HOME WITHOUT A DOG
IS MERELY A SHELTER.

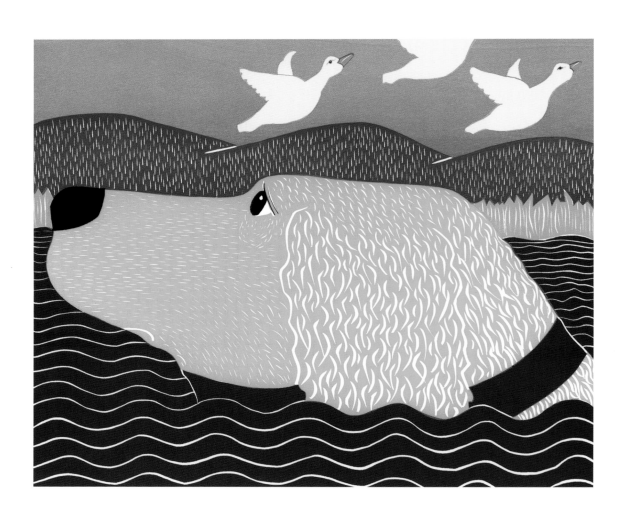

DOGS FIND JOY IN
THE SIMPLEST THINGS.

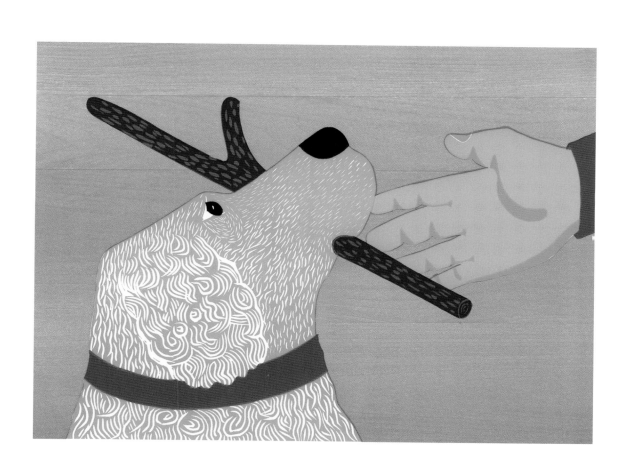

TO BRING YOUR DOG JOY,
PUT ON YOUR JACKET
AND GRAB A LEASH!

THERE IS ONLY ONE THING
A DOG LIKES BETTER THAN
GOING FOR A WALK.

WE CAN'T CHOOSE OUR
PARENTS, BUT WE CAN
CHOOSE OUR FRIENDS.

BE GOOD TO YOUR FRIENDS.

IF YOU TRAVEL A LOT,
BRING A FRAMED PICTURE
OF YOUR DOG TO PUT NEXT
TO YOUR BED. YOU WILL
SLEEP BETTER.

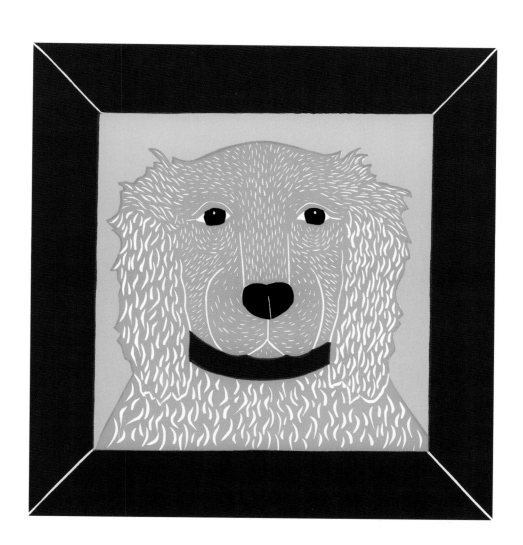

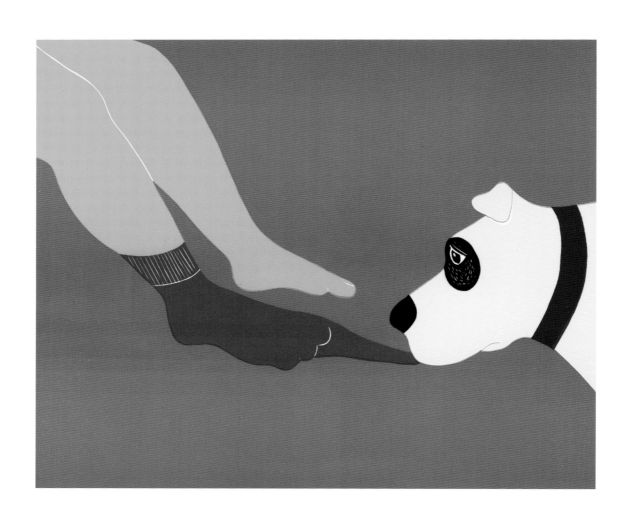

DOGS LOVE TO PLAY.

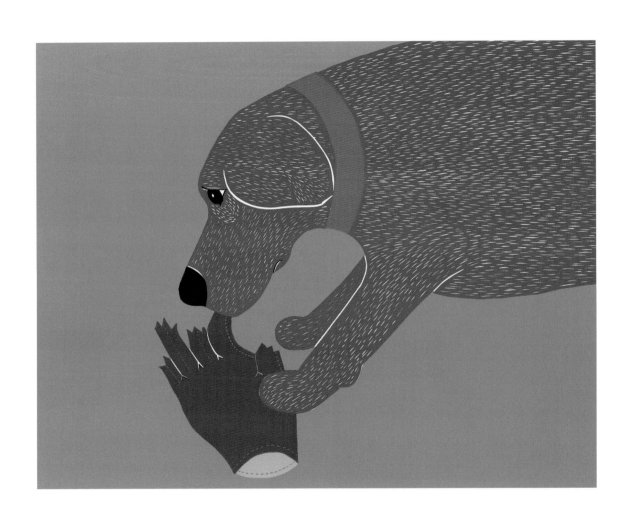

THEY CAN AMUSE
THEMSELVES FOR HOURS.

IF YOU FEEL YOU ARE
TOO OLD TO PLAY,
BUY A BALL AND
A DOG TO GO
WITH IT.

YOU CAN TRUST A DOG
WITH YOUR LIFE...

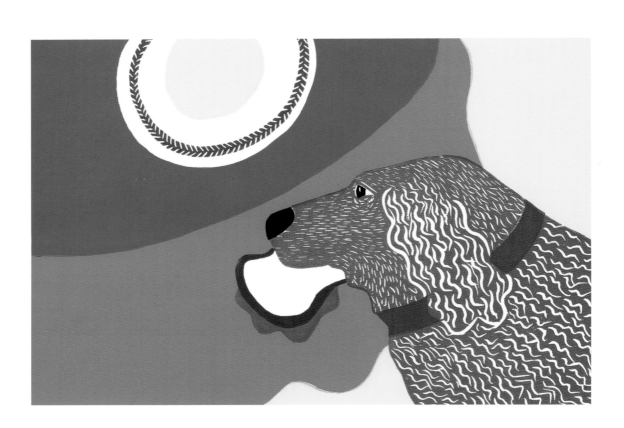

BUT NOT WITH YOUR LUNCH.

DOGS ARE TRUSTING BUT NOT STUPID.

IF YOUR DOG IS YOUR GURU,
YOU COULD DO A LOT WORSE.

THERE'S A LITTLE BIT OF
GOD IN EVERYTHING.

A DOG HAS A SOUL.

A DOG HAS THE SOUL
OF A PHILOSOPHER.
—PLATO

A DOG HAS THE SOUL
OF AN ARTIST.
—HUNECK

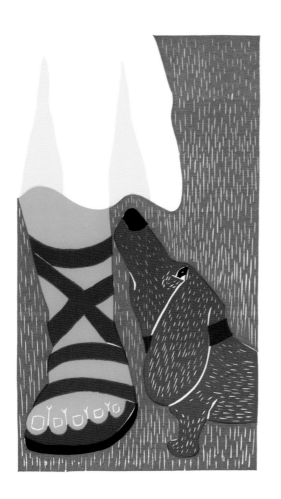

IT HURTS BEYOND WORDS
TO SUFFER THE LOSS
OF A FRIEND.

THE MORE CLEARLY
YOU SEE REALITY,
THE MORE CLEARLY
YOU SEE ANGELS.

HEAVEN IS
PEOPLE SMILING
AND DOGS PLAYING.

WHEN YOU GET TO HEAVEN,
YOUR DOG WILL BE WAITING
TO WELCOME YOU.

YOU TOO CAN BUILD
A CHAPEL IN MEMORY
OF YOUR DOG, IN A PLACE
THAT IS ALWAYS OPEN—
YOUR HEART.

WELCOME
ALL CREEDS,
ALL BREEDS.
NO DOGMAS
ALLOWED.

REMEMBRANCE WALL

Dear Friends,

As part of the Dog Chapel, I have started a Remembrance Wall dedicated to all the animals we have known and loved. Please feel free to add to the wall photos of animals dear to you with any message you wish to write. This is a wonderful way to celebrate the time you spent together and to share it with others.

If you can't visit us in person in Vermont, please feel free to send photos and messages to the following address:

Dog Chapel
1356 Spaulding Road
St. Johnsbury, VT 05819

or E-mail them to us at love@dogchapel.com.

Warmest regards,

LOVE

I'LL ALWAYS REMEMBER THIS ABOUT MY DOG:

interested in having your dogs photograph included in future publications about the Remembrance Wall
pel. please print your name. your dogs name. your street address, and your email address below.

Name: _____

Dogs name: _____

Address: _____

_____

Email: _____